PRODUCT DEMOS THAT SELL

How to Deliver Winning SaaS Demos

Close.io Co-founder & CEO, Steli Efti

PRODUCT DEMOS THAT SELL

Steli Efti

Copyright © 2015

Close.io, Elastic Inc.

Published by Close Publishing
501 Forest Ave
Palo Alto, CA 94301
www.close.io

Cover by Close.io

ISBN-10: 151770782X
ISBN-13: 978-1517707828

DEDICATION

To my mother Anthoula, my wife Diana, and my little super
hustlers Georgios and Leonidas.

CONTENTS

INTRODUCTION

Why do I care about giving good product demos? What qualifies me to write a book about it?

I started a company originally called ElasticSales and our team helped over 200 venture-backed startups in Silicon Valley develop predictable and scalable sales models.

In the process, we gave thousands of product demos ourselves. All of the companies we did sales for sold B2B SaaS products and so we always had to do product demos and webinars.

Not only did we give demos for hundreds of different products, we watched thousands of demos from other companies. Every time someone wanted to work with us, we had them give us a product demo and we would join a few product demos with real customers and prospects to see how they were doing it.

I can honestly tell you that I have seen too much painful shit, having gone through too many bad demos. And I have made it my personal mission to stop this and to make the world give better product demos.

That's why the first chapter of this book is dedicated to all of the bad demos out there while the rest of the chapters show you how to demo the right way, from start to finish.

With this book, you'll spend less time giving boring, irrelevant demos and more time creating value and closing deals.

Steli Efti, CEO of Close.io

THE SEVEN DEADLY SINS OF DEMOING

This book is for sales reps and founders that want to sell their software.

If you are going to get the most value out of this book, you have to be actively engaged every step of the way.

Having been on both the receiving and giving end of countless product demos, I have seen the same mistakes, again and again.

That's why I want you to go through this list of the seven deadly sins of demoing and see if you have committed any of them.

1. You give too many product demos

I join a product demo to a prospect that a founder, CEO, or junior salesperson gives. It's a one-hour demo and at the end of 60 minutes of talking:

Sales rep: "All right, what's your opinion on this? Do you like it?"

Prospect: "That was cool. Thank you so much."

Sales rep: "No, no, wait—are you interested in buying? What's the next step?"

Prospect: "Oh no, I'm just a student and I'm doing some research. Thanks again, this was really helpful."

Holy shit! Did nobody qualify this person before you gave them an hour of your time and effort?

The problem is that too many product demos are being given to people who are not truly qualified!

No offense to all the students out there, but as a sales rep, your time is too valuable for that shit. You can't waste it by giving a product demo to every Tom, Dick, and Harry out there. Selectivity is your friend when qualifying prospects.

2. You haven't sold the demo

One of the biggest mistakes that teams and companies make is they don't sell the demo!

Sales rep: "Oh, I think this is a perfect fit. The next step will be to give you a product demo. I will send you an email and let's find the time next week to do a 60-minute product demo."

Prospect: "Oh, okay."

(Next week, the prospect looks at their schedule and decides, "I'm really busy right now. I don't have enough time to attend a product demo.")

Without fail, every week, people ask me "Why do we have such a high rate of no-shows for our product demo?"

It's not enough to invite prospects to a demo—you actually have to sell the demo!

3. You mistake product demos for training tools

Demos are sales tools, period. Too many people give product demos as if they are product training sessions.

Here's the difference: when you give a demo, you help a prospect understand the value your product can generate for them and you help them make a buying decision. It's sales.

Once somebody is a customer, you might want to give them training on how to become proficient in using your product and getting the maximum value out of it.

3

However, until the prospect becomes a customer, you're selling, not training.

4. Your demos are too long

Since people confuse product demos for training tools (see sin #3), demos are way too long!

The average product demo is 60 minutes. Nobody can remember 60 minutes of product features and "if you click on this button ... ".

The prospect doesn't know your product and hasn't used it. Show them the most valuable things and get going with it.

We'll discuss the ideal length of a product demo later in the chapter "How to Give Product Demos", but just know that it is *not* 60 minutes.

5. You demo features, instead of value

The purpose of your product demo is demonstrate value, not features and functionalities.

Nobody cares about your product's features. What that means is that when you're giving your product demo, you need to focus on how your product is going to help your prospect:

- create value
- save time
- increase revenue
- solve problems

Don't show the prospect a list of features; they don't care yet.

The prospect simply wants to know if the product is good and how it's going to make their life better.

Skip the clicks and get to the point.

6. You failed to capture the prospect's attention at the most important point

If you give a demo and you give it remotely—meaning you can't see eye to eye with the person because they're not in the same room as you—you have to highlight the precise moment when prospects need to pay full attention to you.

During a virtual demo, the prospect might be on Facebook or checking their emails, which means you can't assume that you have their full attention the entire time.

Instead, assume that you have very little of people's attention. While giving shorter demos will help keep prospects engaged, it's still important to directly command their attention when you need it most.

Don't let prospects figure out the most important moments on their own; *tell* them when the most important moments are.

7. You don't end the demo with a close

Sales rep (after an hour of demoing): "Thank you for time. I'm glad we were able to discuss the product and that I was able to answer your questions. Have a good day!"

Prospect: "Thanks! You have a good day, too."

Where's the fucking close?

Too many demos don't have a close. They end with no purpose, no direction, no conversion, no "this is the next step I want you to take."

Obviously, this is a major issue. Product demos are sales tools; if they aren't ending in closes or call-to-actions, they are being wasted.

Use the tools you have to get the results you want.

Learn smarter

This list is by no means exhaustive, but it highlights the most common, and deadliest, mistakes I see when sales rep or founders give product demos.

You can spend years learning by trial and error—or you can take a shortcut by learning directly from my experiences.

By presenting the most common mistakes front and center, my aim is to make you more self-aware as you read this book, allowing you to get the most value from it.

Now that you have a better idea of the areas you need to work on, let's get started with the first step of giving a product demo: qualifying demo attendees.

PRODUCT DEMO DISCOVERY: QUALIFYING DEMO ATTENDEES

Why is qualifying demo attendees so important? Because it will help you understand which features to show your prospect and how to craft a product demonstration that connects with your audience and excites them. You'll be able to map your product's benefits to your prospect's needs.

Research by Sales Benchmark Index has shown that demos conducted without discovering need win 73% less often in a competitive opportunity, whereas companies that tie back their demos to specific pain points are 35% more likely to win the deal.

On the subject of product demos, Robert Falcone, the author of *Just F*cking Demo!*, believes:

> A well prepared demo is obvious. It can be interrupted multiple times. It can be fast-forwarded and rewinded without flustering the speaker. It only shows off what the audience needs to see to come to a decision. It's fluid and flexible and—while it may have been obsessively rehearsed—it comes off as effortless.

How could you possibly conduct a successful demo if you don't know the prospect's evaluation criteria?

Without qualifying, you can only deliver a one-size-fits-all demo. (If you've ever worn one-size-fits-all clothing, you know there's really no such thing.)

Customize your product demo to your prospect's desired results to make the most out of your sales opportunities.

Research prospects before qualifying them

Spending a couple of minutes (or more, if it's a deal crucial to your company) to gather some information about the prospect can help you gain more valuable insights when talking with them.

Learn about:

- Their customers: Through testimonials, case studies and customer logos.
- Their team: Through "About Us" pages, LinkedIn profiles, and blog posts.
- Their partners: They often display partnerships on the website.

Another way to research a company is by looking them up through business research companies like Dun & Bradstreet or Hoovers, but for most startups, this won't be necessary.

When should you qualify them?

It's best to qualify prospects before you even set the appointment for a demo. Assuming a prospect expressed interest in a demo, and you're on the phone with that person, just say:

"I want to make sure that we don't waste any of your time on a demo that doesn't answer your questions and provide you with the insights you need to make an informed decision. That's why I'm going to ask you a few questions about your interest in our software."

Then, proceed to ask questions.

You can, of course, also dedicate the first minutes of your demo to this. However, it's a good idea to do this in a separate conversation because you might discover that you're not a good fit for that prospect, thus saving yourself and your prospect time spent scheduling a demo that won't provide any value.

Know your audience

If multiple people are attending your demo, ask each one to introduce themselves. There are three pieces of information that are particularly useful to you:

- What's their job title?
- What's their main responsibility?
- What insights do they hope to gain from attending your demo?

Questions you want answered

Ideally you want to create your own list of questions that work best for your sales needs, but here are some questions to get you started:

- Why is the prospect interested in your solution?
- Which objectives do they hope your product will help them achieve?
- Which problems do they hope your product will help them solve?
- How are they currently trying to achieve this?
- What do they like most about their current approach?
- What do they dislike most about their current approach?
- What do they want improved?
- Have they used a similar product in the past (or are they currently)?
- What other products are they evaluating?
- Who are the stakeholders involved in the deal?
- How do they feel about your product? What are their individual objectives, objections, wants, and needs?
- How are they evaluating your solution, which KPIs do they want your product to push?

It's worth investing some time upfront into formulating a set of questions.

Types of questions

The effectiveness of the questions you ask depends upon which type of questions you ask.

Open-ended questions: These are questions which require an answer that's more than just a "yes" or a "no". The majority of your qualifying questions should be open-ended, as they tend to elicit the most insightful responses.

Closed questions: Closed questions are questions that can be answered with either a "yes" or a "no". During the qualification stage, they are most useful when you want to make sure that you've understood a prospect's statement correctly. Use them infrequently.

Why questions: Asking "why" will reveal a prospect's beliefs and motivations. If a prospect tells you that they need to be able to split test email campaigns, ask them why that's important to them. This might yield insights into critical business issues that will play an important part in their decision-making process.

The types of questions you ask should also be targeted to the audience you're speaking to.

If you're demoing to end-users:

- What's their workweek like?
- What do they spend time on?
- What are the processes they repeatedly go through?
- Where are they frustrated with these processes?
- What results do they want from a tool?

11

The answers to these questions can help you match their workflows with your product's features. This will also help *them* make a clear connection between your product and how it applies to their jobs.

Generally, the questions you ask when you're speaking to end-users of your software should be more focused on tactical issues, whereas when you're talking with high-level executives, you want to focus your questions on strategy.

Are their answers meaningful?

Sometimes, prospects will give you obvious answers. A problem that's especially common among so-called "veteran" sales professionals is that they accept these answers.

Sales rep: "What do you hope to gain from using our software?"

Prospect: "We want to increase revenue."

Sales rep: "Ok, great, our software can help you do that!"

What??? Of course they want to increase revenue. But how much do they want to increase it by? What are they currently making? Are their revenues growing, steady, or declining? Most importantly, why do they think your product might help them achieve their goal?

Developing your analysis and assessment skills is one of the most important things you can do to become more successful in sales.

Bob Riefstahl shares a great method for eliciting meaningful answers in his book, *Demonstrating to Win! The Indispensable Guide for Demonstrating Software*:

I always, always, always ask each individual, "If it was completely up to you, what three things would you change about your existing system?" Then ask, "What are the three best things about your existing system?" If appropriate, ask, "What are the three things you'd like demonstrated when I come back?" Basically, these are three ways of asking the same question, right? Why ask it three different ways? I've found if I only ask one question, I get responses like, "I would like the system to be much faster." Sure, better response time will be a nice thing to highlight, but you need to dig deeper. Two or three variations of the same question will uncover real issues. You will get truly meaningful information.

Feature/need matrix

For substantial deals where you have plenty of insights into the prospects' wants and needs, you can even create a matrix to map their needs against your features.

Just rate how important each feature is for your prospect on a scale of 0 to 10 (0 = completely irrelevant, 10 = they absolutely want this and no deal will happen if this isn't fulfilled).

Feature 1:   6
Feature 2:   2
Feature 3:   9

Very simple, yet useful.

Know which features not to demo

Qualifying is as much about learning which features you should skip, as it is about which features you should demonstrate. If a feature isn't relevant to a prospect's objectives, don't demo it.

"Demonstrating isn't a contest of more; it's a contest of more relevant."—Bob Riefstahl

Great demos aren't about showing off every bell and whistle your product has to offer—it's all about creating a vision for the prospect of how your product can make their lives better.

Balancing ideal and real

In an ideal world, you'd have extensively qualified every single demo attendee prior to delivering your demo. In the real world, sometimes this is not possible because prospects won't provide you with a lot of information upfront, or it's cost prohibitive for you to spend hours discovering your prospects' needs.

We've covered relatively extensive methods of qualifying demo attendees and leave it up to you to decide how far you want to take it.

For lower contract value prospects, or in cases where you are already familiar with the industry and similar clients, you can often make educated guesses about the priorities of the prospects, without having to go through a lengthy qualification process. If you're at that stage, you're best equipped to make that judgment call yourself. If you're just beginning, putting more effort into qualifying your prospects is time well-spent.

Properly qualifying a prospect will help you show your software in the best possible light. You want to create a vision of how your solution will make their lives better, and in order to do so, you need to know what they most care about.

HOW TO SCHEDULE PRODUCT DEMO APPOINTMENTS

Once you've decided whether a prospect is a fit, look at it from their point of view. Why should they make time in their busy schedule for this demo? What's in it for them? Why should they do it now? Why should they dedicate their time to you and not another vendor?

If you don't have compelling answers to these questions, you'll miss out on a lot of demo opportunities. It's not enough to invite prospects to a demo. You actually have to deliver a compelling pitch and apply salesmanship so they'll commit to joining your demo.

Sell, but don't be salesy

Here are some reasons that won't convince prospects to attend your product demo:

- You're polite and great at making small talk.
- You can talk a lot about how amazing your product is and can interrupt everything the prospect says with your own great story.
- You tell prospects how great they are and how much you love what their company does (and they can tell by the slick and smooth delivery that you're saying the same thing to every single prospect you talk to).
- You tell them that you'd like to learn more about how they want to use your software.
- You tell them they should attend the demo because your software is great and will boost revenues, reduce costs, increase efficiency, etc.

None of these reasons convey value to your prospects. From their point of view, this is all about you wanting their time. You need to show them otherwise.

How to sell the demo

The qualification has given you insights into the objectives they want to achieve. You can bring these up when pitching the demo:

"You should buy from us because you need X, Y, and Z, and we're the best in the world to do these things. This is going to be a real game changer for you. So there's two ways we can proceed from here: 1) you can do this yourself and figure it out, and I'm pretty confident you'll become a customer or 2) I'll connect you to Kevin (the guy who has helped companies like yours to achieve X, Y and Z even faster with our software), because a 30-minute call with him will get you these results within the next five days."

If a prospect resists at this point, ask them why. One of the most common objections is about time: they don't want to spend half an hour on a demo.

How do you manage this objection?

Attending the demo = saving time

Bring up the value of their time and make that the reason why they should attend the demo.

"Rather than spending hours trying out our software and reading documentation, just spend 30 minutes attending a demo, getting answers to your questions and having a true expert help you customize the product to your specific needs and workflow."

Attending the demo = being more successful

Another common reason why people don't want to attend a demo is that they simply don't see the value in it. Sell them on it by clearly spelling out the value.

"We've found that people who try our software are 35% more likely to succeed with our solution when they join a 30-minute, one-on-one demo. It's the fastest way to figure out if our product can help you, get answers to any questions you have and start using our software in a way that's optimized for your workflow. It'll help you get the most out of this trial."

Set an appointment during the call

Once you get their commitment to attend a demo, schedule the demo right away. Tell them to open up their calendar and suggest a date and time to do the demo.

Waiting until after the call to schedule an appointment over email could result in your email being lost in the prospect's inbox. Leave nothing up to chance.

Invite decision makers

This is part of the qualifying process (and you should never demo to someone you haven't qualified first), but it's worth repeating: make sure that the person you're demoing to is actually the decision-maker, or at least a crucial stakeholder.

If they're not the decision-maker, ask them to invite the decision-maker to join the demo with them.

Re-confirm the appointment

Send the prospect a calendar invite right after the call. Then, send them a reminder a day in advance of the appointed time and get them to confirm. If they don't respond, send them another reminder in the morning.

Get the product demo attendance rates you want

From selling the demo to re-confirming the appointment, following these steps has helped the Close.io sales team achieve very high product demo attendance rates. Almost everyone shows up to our product demos and there's nothing preventing you from experiencing the same turnout as well.

HOW TO PREPARE FOR GIVING PRODUCT DEMOS

We've already covered how to schedule more demo appointments with qualified prospects.

Now, we're going to talk about the possibly most unglamorous part of giving demos: the nuts and bolts of preparing demos that turn into sales.

Thorough preparation will help you create and deliver effective product demonstrations and improve your close rates.

Know your demo tools

If you're giving remote demos using an online presentation tool, learn how the software works. Use their training materials, read their documentation, and do a test demo with a colleague to familiarize yourself with the behavior of the software.

You might think "Duh, of course!"' But attend a couple of live demos; the amount of people who do this for a living, yet can't handle the tools they use professionally is ridiculous.

Here's a couple of things you should do:

- Try different hardware setups on the client side (e.g. what will your screen share demonstration look like when the other party views it on a 13-inch notebook screen versus a 27-inch monitor?).
- Is there any lag or delay?
- If you're giving them remote access to your app, how will the app behave?
- What's the experience like when using annotations in your screen share software?
- Is your desktop clean and tidy, or cluttered with personal files?

Hardware

Invest in a good headset. Don't use the built-in microphone in your laptop, a $20 Bluetooth device, or even a speakerphone.

The Internet will screw up the audio quality of your call bad enough, so do everything you can to ensure the best sound quality possible on your end.

If your prospect has trouble understanding what you say, it'll be very difficult to hold their attention.

Haven't demoed your product in a while?

If you're not on top of your demo game (or this is the very first time you've ever delivered a demo of this product), then by all means practice first!

Do a full run of your demo, from A to Z, for a friend or colleague, pretending they're a customer.

Have some lines ready

If, not when, there's a technical glitch, the last thing you want to do is think about what to say. That's why it's good to prepare.

If your app suddenly crashes during the demo, what will you say? How will you bridge the time it takes to get up and running again?

If your presentation software suddenly starts lagging because of a slow Internet connection, how will you deal with this?

It's good to have a few lines for different scenarios prepared. There's no bonus points for being brilliant on the spot.

If Chris Rock did demos . . .

In fact, learn from the best performers in the world and constantly practice. Calibrate which phrasing gets the best audience reaction. Famous stand-up comedians like Chris Rock practice their gigs hundreds of times with different audiences to gauge their reactions. They're literally split testing jokes to see which ones get the biggest laughs.

Do the same with your demos: experiment with different ways of presenting certain features and see what gets your prospects excited about your software.

Widgets by Acme Inc.

You need some kind of placeholder data when you're demoing your product. A lot of companies will use ACME as a company name, John Smith as a customer name, and Widget A, Widget B, Widget C as product names. That's a bad idea.

If you can, use the kind of data your prospect would be using. This will help them make the connection between your product and their actual work routines.

If entering customized sample data for each prospect isn't feasible, come up with creative ways to still make your sample data stand out.

When we're demoing our inside sales software, one of our sample customers is the Bluth Company (if you're a fan of the show Arrested Development, you'll appreciate the reference).

In one of the sample email exchanges, a banana stand is mentioned (which, again, as a fan of Arrested Development will put a smile on your face).

We reference different movies and parts of popular culture in our sample data, and it often elicits a laugh or positive response from prospects when they notice one of these references.

It's much better than using Widget C by ACME. It's one of those little details that shows you care.

Immediately before the demo

Open the browser tabs, app windows, or pages you'll show your audience during the demo before the demo starts. Have them minimized in the background, so people don't have to watch you navigate to these pages and wait for them to load. This will save you only a few seconds during the demo, but will create a better impression of speed.

If you always use the same setup, simply open all the pages in separate tabs and bookmark them so you can conveniently load them all in the same order for your demos.

Turn off chat notifications, instant messengers, and any other apps that could unexpectedly pop up on the screen and distract your viewers from your demo.

Do you use any browser extensions or toolbars that take up valuable screen space? It's best to launch a new browser without any add-ons and present in full-screen mode. Minimize visual clutter.

Open an empty text file where you can jot down prospect's questions or notes to yourself during the demo. If you already have the window in the background and don't make viewers wait for an app to start, it's just another way of demonstrating that you're a pro.

Hit the record button!

Being able to replay your live demos and review your strengths and weaknesses, especially in the early days of giving demos, is an invaluable tool. There's much to be learned from reviewing your demos without having to be attentive to your prospect, and you'll get plenty of ideas for improving your demo.

Most web presentation solutions offer you an easy option to record you demo. Just double-check that you have enough storage space available, as some providers have pretty strict limits.

I'd advise against using a screen-recorder that you've installed on your system. They can bring system performance down and occasionally, there are issues when using them in combination with screen sharing software.

But if you do use a screen-recorder, by all means do a test-run for the same period of time with the same setup you'll use during the demo. You might think testing two minutes of screen-recording will give you all the insights you need, but 30 minutes into your live demo, the software may slow down your system or simply crash.

Have an agenda

Decide in advance the three things you want your demo audience to remember about your product.

I'm sure there's more you will want them to remember, and there definitely will be more that you'll show them. But if you assume that they could remember only three things, what are the three things you'd want your product demo attendees to remember? What are the highlights you want to highlight?

Prepare now, relax later

Once you've got a great demo-win rate, you'll be fine without meticulous preparation for your demos. However, being well-prepared and familiarizing yourself with the process, especially when you're just getting started, can make the difference between feeling confident and professional or insecure and incompetent.

HOW TO GIVE PRODUCT DEMOS

It's showtime!

Actually deliver a great demo that will turn prospects into buyers.

In this chapter, you'll learn how to:

- structure and open your demo
- apply the rules of effective demo engagement
- deliver a compelling presentation
- deal with the various scenarios you will encounter when demoing to a prospect
- ensure your three most important points stick
- and finally, close the demo

Let's get to it!

How to structure your demos

Structuring successful demos is something you'll get better at with experience. The more often you do this, the sharper your instinct will be. But to give you a head start, I'm going to share a general blueprint with you.

An important thing to keep in mind: this is a general blueprint. It's solid, but as with everything, there are many possible exceptions. If you have a good reason to structure your demos differently, by all means, do so!

I'd rather have you experiment with ten different ways of structuring your demo and fail nine times but learn a lot, than dogmatically stick to one sequence just because I said so.

I'm giving you a way of thinking about structuring your demos, more than an actual demo blueprint. It's a bit more work, but more valuable to you if you apply the lessons to your own demos.

What are the three most important points of your pitch?

Before you go into a pitch, think about the three most important things you want your prospect to realize and remember about your offer.

Sales pitches with three positive claims are the most persuasive according to the study "When Three Charms But Four Alarms: Identifying the Optimal Number of Claims in Persuasion Settings":

> In settings where consumers know that the message source has a persuasion motive, the optimal number of positive claims is three. More claims are better until the fourth claim, at which time consumers' persuasion knowledge causes them to see all the claims with skepticism.—Kurt Carlson and Suzanne Shu

This is the single most important takeaway from this whole chapter. If you could only do one thing, do this from now on: whenever you go into a pitch, take a couple of moments to prepare and be very clear about the three main points you want to make—these will be the highlights of your sales pitch. What are the three things that will make the biggest impact on prospects?

Always go from macro to micro

When you're demoing a feature, always give your prospects the big picture first. They should never watch you demo something and be unsure of its purpose.

If a prospect wonders "Why is this guy showing me this?", then you haven't properly explained what you're going to demonstrate.

"You've said that you need a better way of managing your sales pipeline, because right now it's a mess from always manually

31

scheduling these tasks. We've solved this problem for you—I can show you how to automate your pipeline management, so you won't have to deal with manual task reminders anymore. Does that sound interesting to you?"

By doing this, you achieve three things:

- You give them context for what you're about to show them, and help them understand how they will benefit from this.
- You've engaged them by making them speak.
- You've confirmed that the feature you'll demonstrate is actually relevant to them, ensuring you make the best use of the time you have with your prospect.

The product demo is not the time to bombard prospects with minutiae. You're the expert on your product and if you play your cards right, your prospect-turned-customer will also become an expert. However, before you can reach that moment, remember:

Reveal your capabilities in layers, in accord with the customer's level of interest.... First, show the route to achieve the desired result with the fewest number of mouse clicks (the "Do It" pathway). This proves your capabilities and helps build a vision in your customer's minds: they can visualize themselves using your software. Then, as your customer asks questions, you can drive deeper to show more relevant breadth of the Specific Capabilities desired (the "Peel Back the Layers" pathways). Note that the highest-ranking audience members may only need to see the "Do It" to be convinced.—Peter Cohan, strategy consultant, angel investor, and author

Sketch the big picture first, go into details later.

Which features should you feature?

When you're demoing a product, you always want to demonstrate value, not features or functionalities. Nobody cares about the features of your software—the only thing they care about is what it'll do for them.

> "Your product is only as good as the problems it can solve for someone. What I want to hear during a demo is what problems you are solving and for who[m], not a laundry list of features in your product."—Ryan Leask, Manager of Data Engineering at Facebook

If you've properly qualified prospects and understand their needs, you're in a position to deliver a compelling demonstration rather than throw darts in the dark.

Begin with a big bang

Once you've gotten the introduction and qualifying out of the way, and you start with your actual product demo, it's important to start with something sensational.

> I remember getting my first demo of a spreadsheet in 1979, from Dan Fylstra, the president of Personal Software. Dan understood some of the basics of giving a good demo. Before minute #1 was over, I had seen him enter a new number in one cell and watched the numbers ripple down and to the right. I know it was a great demo and a great product because I still get goosebumps thinking about it! Of course you can't expect to have a product as revolutionary as VisiCalc was in 1979, but there must be something that wows 'em every time. Don't save that for the end. Put it up front where it belongs.—Dave Winer, software developer and author of the blog *Scripting News*

For some reason, I see sales reps "keeping the good stuff for the end". That will backfire most of the time.

If you keep the good stuff for the end, all that's left is the boring stuff for the beginning and the middle—and you'll likely lose your prospect's attention before you even get to the end.

Yes, you should have a great ending, but only after you had a great beginning!

Start with a killer feature of your product that serves an important need for your prospect. Based upon the qualification process, you know what their pain points are, you know where they're itching.

Scratch that itch. Show them how your product resolves a major frustration or helps them achieve their objectives faster, with less effort, and more fun.

"A demo allows the customer to see and feel how things will be better if they buy (and worse if they don't)."—Geoffrey James, author of *The Tao of Programming* and *Business Without the Bullsh*t*

Don't forget to paint a vivid picture in their imagination of how your product can make their lives easier and help them do their jobs better.

> A real demo should start with one of the specific problems or challenges the customer or prospect said they are having. They sound more like this: 'During our previous conversation you stated your team was having a difficult time sharing documents and collaborating was difficult. In this part of the demo we want to show you how you would be able to share documents easier and increase collaboration without breaking your current file structure and maintaining federal compliance.'— Jim Keenan, author of the blog *A Sales Guy*

It's important that this clearly relates to one of their main priorities. It shouldn't be a minor feature or small optimization. This is even more important if you're demoing, not to an end-user, but to someone in a managerial position. They want to see how your software can affect the big picture.

Start off by talking about something in big, general terms before you drill down into specifics. Show them what your software can do for them, then ask them: "Would you like to see how this works, or do you want to move on to the next item?"

Asking them this question keeps them engaged, and you get feedback on how relevant a given feature is to them.

The worst thing you can do is just string together feature after feature, and make your prospect sit through a long parade of things they don't care about.

Rules of effective demo engagement

An effective demo is as much an art as a science. As such, mastering the technical qualifications is only one part; you must also convey competency and passion.

As Maya Angelou eloquently stated, "People will forget what you said, people will forget what you did, but people will never forget how you made them feel." Make your prospects feel great about your product.

Speak their language

If you've noticed while qualifying a prospect that they use certain words and phrases, use those same words and phrases later. Check out their website and see the wording they use on there. Look at previous email exchanges and study the terminology they use. Make an effort to speak their language.

But don't launch into jargon just to appear like a knowledgeable insider. If you use acronyms they don't understand, they usually won't ask you what it means. It's just like in school: nobody wants to be the person that asks the stupid questions.

Handle your mouse like a pro

Keep in mind that people are following your mouse movements. When you want people to see how you're doing something, move your mouse cursor more deliberately than you usually would. No herky-jerky movements, please.

When should you interrupt a prospect during a demo?

A prospect is asking you a long-winded question and before she's halfway through, you already know what her question is. Eager to show her how well you understand her, you jump in and answer the question she's not yet finished.

Wrong! Never interrupt a prospect who is asking a question.

In the worst case, you've made a wrong assumption and answered a question she didn't ask, which will alienate her twice: once because you've cut her off, and again because you've just demonstrated that you absolutely misunderstood her.

Recovering from a blunder like this is tough, so it's better to avoid putting yourself in a tough spot in the first place. And even if you actually answered the right question, nobody likes a know-it-all. Let people finish their sentences.

Answering questions with questions

Sometimes the best way to answer a prospect's question is by flipping it around on them.

Prospect: "Well, how does your software handle lead

assignments?"

Sales rep (puffing his chest because he sees a chance to show off a cool feature of his product): "Oh, leads are automatically assigned to a rep based on the parameters you entered!"

Prospect: "Yeah, we've tried that in the past, that really destroyed our numbers."

That didn't go well, did it?

Now, let's look how the same dialogue could have played out, if our rep had flipped the question.

Prospect: "How does your software handle lead assignments?"

Sales rep: "I love that you ask that question, because that's one of the things our customers really like about our software. Now tell me, how do you want your software to handle lead assignments?"

Prospect: "We've had this semi-automated system, and it really messed up our numbers. We found that this is one of the areas where it's really worth manually reviewing and assigning each lead."

Sales rep: "Absolutely, you can do that with our software."

If your software has different options for handling a certain workflow, then it's best to first inquire what the prospect prefers. Many times your product is flexible enough to adapt to their preferred workflow, but if you make assumptions and tout one way as superior, it's hard to step back from that.

Flipping questions is a great way to learn more about the underlying reasons for why a prospect wants things a certain way.

Questions you can't (or don't want to) answer?

Even if you've got serious product expertise, sometimes a prospect will ask you a question for which you don't have an answer. Or a question which would derail your demo if you took the time to answer it.

In these cases, just respond: "That's an interesting question. I have an idea what the answer will be, but I'm not 100% certain. Let me write this question down so I can follow up with you in a day or two about this."

Then, write down their question in a text file, in front of their eyes where they can see it. This will put their minds at ease and provide some closure.

Ask questions that contextualize the value you provide

Let's say you've identified a problem they have, and you have the solution. What you want to do is not just show it to them, but first put it in context.

Sales rep: "So, currently your company is losing out on sales opportunities because leads are falling through the cracks. You've got tasks and notes and reminders in your system for hundreds of leads, and it's just a big mess right now. None of your reps are able to consistently complete the tasks on time and follow up as planned with every lead. That sounds like you're losing out on a lot of potential deals, right?"

Prospect: "That's right, that's why we're looking for a better system now."

Sales rep: "I see. If you had to guess, how much revenue do you think you're missing out on just because of ineffective lead management?"

Prospect: "Well, I haven't really run the math yet, but I'd say roughly $2,000 to $3,000 in deals per rep each month."

Sales rep: "Wow, and you've got 16 reps working for you currently?"

Prospect: "That's right."

Sales rep: "So we're talking hundreds of thousands of dollars in lost deals every year. Well, I'm now going to show you a feature that'll make you hundreds of thousands of dollars over the next twelve months. Do you want to see this?"

You bet she does.

Highlight the highlights

Don't assume you've got your prospect's undivided attention just because they're attending your demo. Especially if you're giving a remote demo, it's almost certain that prospects will multitask during your demo: checking email, Twitter, Facebook, etc.

Knowing this, you want to highlight the highlights and mark what's memorable to ensure you have their attention when it matters the most.

When you reach that critical moment when you really want your prospect to listen, use the prospect's name (if it's a one-on-one demo) and pause for a second.

Tell them this is the most important thing you'll tell them today, make sure they're listening, and then make your point.

Deal with fails, bugs, and crashes

If you give demos on a regular basis, things will go wrong. It's inevitable. Expect it and be prepared for it.

"Oh, I really don't know why this is happening now, I've never seen this before" is not something that will make your demo attendees trust you and your software more.

The worst thing you can do is to allow a bug to throw you off your game. In a later chapter, we'll cover how to turn demo fails into sales.

Requests that are hard to fulfill

Sometimes a request from a prospect is hard to fulfill, or you might not be sure if and how to fulfill it. Here's what you can say in such a case:

"I see this is an issue that we'll have to deal with at some point. Let me write it down so I can follow up with you after discussing this with the right person in our company."

Then, write it down in your demo notes.

Managing time

Managing time is extremely important in order to keep your demos effective. One of the main differences between an amateur and a professional is how they control their time.

An experienced demo pro will complete the demo within the agreed upon timeframe.

An inexperienced person will apologize for going over time until the prospect cuts them off.

If you already know what you want to cover during your demo, set topic start and stop times.

Start your demos on time. If you start late because your prospect is late, confirm that they'll still stay for the same length of time.

If they insist on stopping at the originally scheduled end time, you're still better off knowing that so you can adjust your presentation accordingly, rather than being interrupted midway before you've shown them everything they need to see.

How long should your demos be?

15 minutes or less. Most founders think their software can't be properly demonstrated in 15 minutes, but most demos are way too long.

Do you want to know why?

Because they're confusing product demos with product training.

Product demos ≠ product training

The purpose of a demo isn't to teach your prospects how to use your demo. It's to show your prospects how your product can benefit them.

If you give yourself another 10 to 15 minutes at the end of your demo to answer questions and engage with people, the maximum amount of time you should spend demoing is 30 minutes.

Waiting for a page/feature to load

Let's say there's one function of your app you'd like to show your prospect that takes a few moments to load.

If you know this in advance, the best thing is to already preload it in another tab or window.

If that's not possible, then be prepared for it by having the words ready to mask the delay or ideally, a well-placed question that will prompt them to provide you with some related information.

By the time they've completed their statement, the page has already loaded.

Ensure your 3 most important points stick

At the end of your sales conversation, you will have talked about many different things. How can you make sure that your three most important points still stick in your prospect's mind?

Just ask them one of these questions:

- What were the highlights of this conversation for you?
- I'm wondering, what was the most interesting thing that you've learned in this conversation?
- I want to ask you, in the pitch today, what did you find most impactful? What were the things that you're taking away?
- If somebody asks you tomorrow to describe what we discussed today, how would you summarize our conversation?

The point of asking one of these questions is to close the feedback loop. If they don't talk about your highlights, if they missed something crucial in their answer, then that's an opportunity to highlight the highlights again.

You: "You're absolutely right. The two or three things that you just said are incredibly important. One more thing that I want you to take away is _____."

End with a close

What's your closing statement? It had better be a strong, clear call-to-action. It's your job to get the prospect to take the next step.

I once sat in a pretty awesome demo and was ready to buy on the spot. Then, the guy finishes off like this:

"Thanks for taking the time to learn about our software, I really appreciate it. I hope this has been useful for you, and if you have any further questions at any time, just let me know. Thanks again, have a great day!"

What?

Are you kidding me?

Well, I guess it's not yet time to buy? I'll sleep over this and discuss it with some colleagues (who haven't attended the demo and don't know anything about this product).

Of course, the next day, I've got a thousand other things on my plate, and the deal never happens.

Sell them when they're ready to buy.

Ask them to take out their credit card and sign up now.

At the very least, close them on the next step in the conversion funnel.

Don't waste time—yours or the prospect's—with a generic good-bye.

INCEPTION HACK: INVOLVE THE PROSPECT IN THE DEMO PROCESS

"*Brilliant!*" That's what I thought when I heard Kevin sell this deal.

He was giving a product demo to a prospect, but in a way I've never heard of before, and it ultimately helped to make the sale.

If you're looking for ways to demo your product more effectively, keep reading.

Adapt this approach to your company and you'll transform your product demo into a sales machine.

The neglected little feature I never mentioned during product demos

I've demoed Close.io hundreds of times, but never once did I mention "Opportunities" in our sales software. It's a pretty simple and standard feature, and most sales CRMs have their own version of it.

I've always kept demos focused on the main selling points for the prospect, rather than forcing them to endure an excruciatingly long parade of each and every feature our product has to offer. And our "Opportunities" window never seemed to be important enough.

It's basically a little box that summarizes the main points about an opportunity. You can add a dollar value to the opportunity, a percentage to indicate how confident you are that the deal will close, the estimated date when the deal will close, what the status is, who owns it, whether it's recurring or not, and comments. You can also add multiple opportunities per lead.

It's pretty self-explanatory, and thus, I never brought it up when giving a live product demo.

Turning ordinary features into impressive experiences

Kevin, on the other hand, uses it in his demos. When he's doing the demo, and sharing his screen with the prospect, at some point he tells them:

"Let me show you how this works in action. I'm obviously using Close.io to sell you this deal, and I've got you as a lead. I'm now going to open up your lead page here, so you can see how I'm using Close.io to sell to you."

He then opens up the prospect's page. It displays all of their contact info and the timeline, which includes the complete conversation history via both email and phone, between Kevin and the prospect.

Kevin: "Now, I want you to focus on this box here that's called 'Opportunities'. Tell me, how confident are you that you're going to buy our sales software?"

Prospect: "Probably around 70%."

Kevin: "I'm happy to hear that. This means there's still some work to be done for me to actually win you over, but we're on the right path."

And he moves the confidence level on the screen to 70, while they're watching on their screen.

Kevin: "Now, let's look at the next field: dollar value. How many users do you think you'll buy, and at what level?"

Prospect: "Probably 10 professional users because we want the unlimited U.S. calling from within the app and bulk email."

Kevin: "Great, that'll be around $1,100 a month, right? I can save you $1,320 a year on this if you pay for a year upfront—that's basically more than a free month. Do you want that?"

Prospect: "Sure, makes sense."

Kevin: "So now, you're an opportunity worth $11,880 annually." And he puts that in the opportunity field.

Kevin: "I like what I'm seeing here. Now, let's look at the Estimated Close date. How much time do you think you'll need to make a decision? What needs to happen?"

Prospect: "Well, we just need to make sure the final integration with our internal dashboard works well. We'll do that tomorrow, so we can probably make a decision on Wednesday."

So Kevin takes a note, adds the estimated close date, and clicks the "Save" button.

Kevin: "As you can see, you're now an $11,880 annual opportunity with a 70% chance of closing by Wednesday, depending upon the integration with your internal dashboard. Now, how can we work together to make this opportunity real, to close this deal and make this a success?"

Produce product demos Hollywood-style

This is brilliant! He's selling them our sales software by showing them how to sell with our sales software, and the example he's using is their very own lead page, which he's updating in front of their eyes.

It's like sales meets the movie *Inception*!

And rather than positioning himself as sales person against the prospect (like many pushy sales people), he turns this into a joint effort. Both parties are invested in making it happen.

It's almost exciting to be invited behind the curtain and see how a company that's selling to you is doing it, what data and notes they have on you, and their internal process.

We usually don't get to see these kinds of things and thus, it creates a special and unique experience for the prospect. By doing it this way, it creates an almost irresistible sense of curiosity—you want to see how we're selling to you.

And because we're not hiding anything from the prospect, we're building trust in the sales process.

Why didn't I think of this?

It seemed obvious once I thought about it, and it made me wonder: *what else am I missing?*

It's a good question to ask yourself regularly: What is something you could easily do that would improve your performance, but you're not doing it because you simply haven't thought of it yet?

How can you use this in your product demos?

Unless you're selling sales software, you probably can't apply this directly to your business. But how could you apply this principle to your product demos?

How can you transparently involve the prospect in the process for your own product?

How can you make your product demos more engaging and

inclusive?

What were some highlights you've experienced when receiving a demo?

Try to think outside of the box. You never know what amazing product demo hacks are hiding right underneath your nose, simply waiting to be discovered.

TURN PRODUCT DEMO FAILS INTO SALES

I was demoing a product to a person I've been following for a long time already. Not just some random prospect—someone very accomplished, whom I've looked up to for a long time. Let's just call him Mr. Mysterious.

Just as I was getting into the groove of the demo, a red bar appeared on the screen with an error message. What to do?

How should you proceed when you're giving a product demo, and you're really eager to close the deal, and then your product fails in front of the prospect?

The single biggest mistake you can make during a demo fail is exactly what most people do during a demo fail!

Fumbling around like an amateur

They get thrown off their game and desperately hope things will go back to normal.

They click around and try to assure the prospect that they will fix the product: "Hmm, wait, I think this will just takes a moment." Click, click, click.

"Uh, let me go back here, and try this again." Click, click. Wait.

"Umm, this is embarrassing. Let me log out and log back in again, that should do it." Click, click, click, clack, clack, clack.

Click, click. Nothing.

"Umm, you know . . . well . . . I think we should, uh, reboot the system. One moment here, I'm going to invite you again in a couple of minutes."

Then, they try to bridge the waiting time with a bunch of senseless small talk, trying to appear calm while their tension turns into anxiety.

Stress is contagious

When the sales person is nervous, the prospect often picks up their agitation.

Do you think that uneasiness is a mental state which helps you close deals? Of course it won't—people put up a wall when they're feeling stressed.

In order to make them feel relaxed, you need to be relaxed first.

"This has never happened before."

Almost everybody says that when a demo fails. Almost nobody believes it.

Even if you have never encountered that particular bug before, you surely have dealt with failures and crashes and outages before. So don't act as if this is the first-time, ever.

Every experienced professional knows things go wrong.

Remember Murphy's law: Anything that can go wrong, will go wrong.

There's a reason why this law is popular in the IT field.

From failed demo to fortunate deal

How should you respond when your product fails during a demo? Take a step back and think how you can turn this into an opportunity to connect with your prospect and demonstrate the strengths of your company.

Rather than staying focused on this single occurrence of a bug, make it about something bigger. Here's how I turned a disaster into a deal with Mr. Mysterious when that red error bar popped up on the screen.

Step 1: Instead of stuttering and mumbling, show enthusiasm!

I told him: "See, this is the most important part of the demo. I didn't plan for this, but I'm glad it happened. I'm going to show you what we do when things go wrong."

Step 2: Re-focus on the big picture

"Our app is pretty reliable. We process over 300,000 calls on Close.io every single month, and millions of emails are being sent and received on our platform. We growing rapidly all around the world. Thousands and thousands of sales people rely on us every single day. A lot of them are heavy users who spend many hours every day making calls."

Step 3: Disarm them with honesty

"We're a crucial piece of software. We deliver on that promise but we're also realistic, and acknowledge that once a while something might go wrong."

Step 4: Walk them through your support experience

"We take this responsibility very serious, and that's why we're always here for you. Let's go through this together. You click on the little 'Help' button. Do you want to contact us by email? Our average response time is between two to three hours. But if you want immediate help, go into our support chat."

"These are not some outsourced support agents. These are the engineers who built the product! Not some agent who will look through a database of prewritten answers, but someone with the technical expertise to understand, analyze and resolve your issue. So let's do this together now."

Step 5: Unleash the support beast

In the support chat, our Product Lead guy was able to fix the issue right away.

Step 6: Explicitly spell out the value

"Mr. Mysterious, I hope you see how dedicated we are to taking care of our customers. How many companies will actually go to that extent? We can't promise you that everything will always be perfect. Nobody can. But we'll always be ready to fix any issue you have. You'll always have access to us."

Bonus: Be playful!

If you can have some fun with it, do so. In this case, I was making a joke out of the fact that the prospect would chat directly with the engineer who was responsible for the bug—and that if he couldn't fix it, he'd be out of a job. (Real CEO-humor!)

If it gets your prospect to laugh, that's funny enough. It helps to get rid of any tension.

In fact, the exact sequence of steps you take during a demo fail aren't that crucial. These six steps are just one example of how you can turn a product demo into a sales opportunity.

What's more important than the exact wording or sequence you use is the state you're in. You need to be calm and collected, not falling apart. The message you want to implicitly convey is: This isn't a big deal, it can easily be fixed.

Be the kind of company people want to do business with

Mr. Mysterious ended up buying. Not despite the bug, but because of how we handled it.

He had witnessed firsthand how level-headed we remained when things went down.

Demonstrate that you're going to have clarity and focus, and fix the issue promptly.

When was the last time you had to deal with a demo fail?

Think back to the last time you were demoing your product, and something bad happened.

- How did you handle it?
- Did you react emotionally, or did you handle the problem professionally?
- What could you have done better?

Replay this event in your mind, but re-write the script so that next time, you've already trained your mental muscles to handle demo fails like a seasoned pro.

5 STEPS FOR STARTUPS TO RE-ENGAGE PAST DEMOS & CLOSE LOST PROSPECTS

This chapter was contributed by Lincoln Murphy from Sixteen Ventures. Check out his blog on SaaS growth at http://www.sixteenventures.com.

When it comes to sales hustle, Steli is the man. He's taught us about the power of the follow-up and turning failed demos into sales.

Well, this powerful sales hack I'm going to share takes both of those ideas and applies it to the reality of rapid startup product evolution.

Your product today versus 9 months ago

Look, you're in a startup and that means your product is rapidly changing, evolving from week to week, and sometimes day to day.

You're proud of what you have today (though it's always a work in-progress) and you think back 3 months . . . 6 months . . . OMG, 9 months ago . . . and you shiver at the thought of what your product used to be.

Ugh, yuck.

And then it hits you: you showed that product to prospects back then. A lot of prospects.

Yeah, some of them—the crazy ones who could see the value in spite of your efforts—bought.

But a lot of prospects didn't. And now, those people are walking around with what they think is an accurate picture of your product in their head but that picture is out-of-date.

The product wasn't ready for them and they weren't ready for it, but things are different now.

If they saw your product back then and haven't seen it since, then they really haven't seen your product AT ALL, and they need to. Now.

If they're still in business, then there are just two things that could have happened since they saw your demo or dropped out of the sales cycle with you:

1. Nothing (so they're totally still an opportunity).
2. They signed with a competitor. (Learn why and see if they might still be interested in a demo to see what they're missing. You never know.)

You have absolutely NOTHING to lose by reaching out to past demos or lost prospects and a TON to gain, even if it's just intel on a competitor they ended up going with—and when their contract ends!

5 steps to win back lost deals

The how-to on this is super-simple. It's really one of those things that is all in the execution. Just do it!

1. Get a list consisting of either prospects someone on your team gave a demo to, or prospects who were in a sales cycle with you three, six, or nine months ago (whichever timeframe makes sense for you).
2. Send them an email or call them with a message along the lines of "If you haven't seen [Our Product] in the past x months ... you haven't seen [Our Product]!!"
3. This isn't the time to be coy or shy. You need to be clear that the product they saw back then is NOT the product

you sell today. For this campaign, we're running counter to the typical "make it about them" message we typically employ. This is about your product and why their vision of the product is super-outdated.

4. Set up the appointment and prep for the demo.
5. Set up a reminder (or automated campaign) to reach out every day (or week or month ... whatever you can handle) when a new cohort enters the "got a demo > x months ago" or "lost 'em > x months ago" since, as a startup, your product will always be much different "x" months later.

This works, no excuses. Make Steli proud.

3 EPIC PRODUCT DEMOS (AND WHAT YOU CAN LEARN FROM THEM)

Stand on the shoulders of giants.

Learn from these three demo masterpieces and see how you can bring their ideas and techniques into your own repertoire.

The original Walkman

On July 1st, 1979, Sony "changed the way people listen to music" by introducing the first Walkman. (Sounds familiar?)

Up until that point, unless you carried a boom box around, you simply couldn't walk on the streets and listen to your own music. People didn't wear headphones in public, since Japanese society (which is where the Walkman was first launched) disapproved of it.

How do you launch a product that's completely unknown and up against a negative cultural bias?

Rather than presenting the Walkman to the public in a conference room, the Sony team invited journalists to the Sony building.

Each journalist got a Walkman. Then, a Sony employee would escort them to a bus that drove them to a large park. There, the journalists were told to push the play button on their Walkman.

The cassette had an explanation of what the Walkman was, and asked the journalists to look at various demonstrations of the Walkman at different times.

Sony promoters rode around on roller skates, skateboards and bicycles while wearing their Walkmans, and all of them wore "Walkman" t-shirts.

However, sales were initially slow.

Sony's marketing people decided to have promoters go out and mingle with the public while listening to music on a Walkman. They demoed the product directly to end-consumers and offered Walkmans to young people to try out.

Once people experienced the Walkman listening experience, their skepticism turned into enthusiasm. Sony sent promoters to college and high school festivals, and told retailers to let people try out Walkmans in stores.

Sony also published photographs of young pop stars with Walkmans in magazines, which helped to change public perceptions of wearing headphones in public.

There's no video for the Walkman demo. However, it's a valuable lesson that sometimes, the best way to demo a product is to put it in the hands of the end-user.

Ron Popeil's infomercials

Infomercials are essentially product demos. Ron Popeil has moved billions of dollars in merchandise with his infomercials. He's one of the pioneers of the industry, and if it doesn't completely fry your brain, watch his 30-minute Rotisserie infomercial ("Set it and forget it.").

Are these infomercials ridiculous? Of course they are. But they're also very effective at demonstrating the benefits of the product, keeping the audience engaged, and placing powerful calls-to-action throughout their demos.

As Malcom Gladwell explains in "The Pitchman", an article on Ron Popeil, one component of Popeil's success is his ability to make the product the star:

The rules of pitching [are not] the same as the rules of celebrity endorsement. When Michael Jordan pitches McDonald's hamburgers, Michael Jordan is the star. But when Ron Popeil . . . pitched, say, the Chop-O-Matic, his gift was to make the Chop-O-Matic the star. It was, after all, an innovation. It represented a different way of dicing onions and chopping liver: it required consumers to rethink the way they went about their business in the kitchen. Like most great innovations, it was disruptive. And how do you persuade people to disrupt their lives? Not merely by ingratiation or sincerity, and not by being famous or beautiful. You have to explain the invention to customers—not once or twice but three or four times, with a different twist each time. You have to show them exactly how it works and why it works, and make them follow your hands as you chop liver with it, and then tell them precisely how it fits into their routine, and, finally, sell them on the paradoxical fact that, revolutionary as the gadget is, it's not at all hard to use.

We're obviously not recommending you use the gimmicky infomercial format when selling your SaaS product to B2B prospects. However, studying their methods and understanding what makes them so effective can help you design demos that close more deals.

Amazon Kindle

Upon its release on November 19, 2007, the first version of Amazon's e-book reader sold out in five and a half hours.

There were predictions the Kindle would fail. The earliest e-book reader, the Rocket eBook, was launched in 1998 by NuvoMedia. Subsequent e-book readers would appear, such as the Softbook Reader, EveryBook Reader, and Sony's LIBRIé, but they all flopped.

Reviewing the Kindle, Peter Mortensen, the former communications lead for the firm Jump Associates, observed:

> In terms of basic usability, it's an absolute bear. The page-turn buttons are awkwardly located, and the display can be very slow to update when you flip a page or browse Amazon over the wireless connection. For pure reading experience, the Sony eReader is a better design.

What the Kindle lacked design-wise, it made up for with:

- A larger selection of e-books available for downloading (an issue that was a large stumbling block for other e-book reader companies).
- The ability to download content directly to the device without syncing to a computer.
- Free "WhisperNet" 3G data connection, which could be used to download content and browse the web.

The two-minute introductory video for the Amazon Kindle can still be viewed online. After highlighting the features and benefits of the Kindle, the narrator ends with a value proposition that encapsulated the Kindle's convenient, yet groundbreaking, nature: "Amazon Kindle, read what you want, anywhere, any time with Amazon's revolutionary wireless reading device."

Like Ron Popeil, Amazon made the device the star of the show (without the flashiness). This technology is commonplace now, but when Amazon released the Kindle in 2007, it was spectacular. Make your demo spectacular as well.

Find inspiration anywhere

It's a good idea to study a wide variety of fields when it comes to giving effective product demos. Expose yourself to different styles of demoing a product and see how you can adapt them to your own software presentations. The best minds are able to take information and ideas from anywhere, and create something unique and valuable in return.

Why You Need Our Awesome Sales Software

Let's get something out of the way first: CLOSE.IO IS NOT FOR EVERYONE!

If you are:

- Managing a pipeline of less than 100 leads per year
- Not using a phone or email to do sales
- Currently working for a Fortune 500 Company

You SHOULDN'T buy Close.io. It's not you, it's us (wink).

Don't worry, if you email me (Steli@close.io) and tell me this is not for you, I will personally send you recommendations for other sales software that will help you be more successful. I know them all. No problem.

Now, here are four reasons why Close.io will help you close more deals and make more sales.

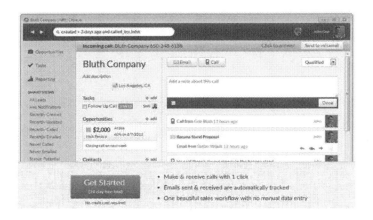

1. You can finally say NO to data entry

We hate data entry as much as you do, so we tried our hardest to help you avoid it. With auto-logging of calls, emails, and activity, you can spend more time closing deals instead of entering data.

2. You will make more, and better, calls

Make and receive calls with just 1-click. All calls are logged automatically. Lead activity information pops up as soon as the phone rings, so the data you need is always at your fingertips!

3. You will send more, and better, emails

All your sales-related emails are automatically tracked within the app, no matter where you write the emails. You can also see who opened your emails, save templates to improve your email workflow, and keep all digital sales communication in one place without any manual work.

4. You can get answers to all your questions

The Close.io app collects most data based on your actual behavior, and thus has not only more data, but also more accurate sales data. We've built a powerful search platform that allows you to answer any question within seconds.

Example? "Show me all leads in California with a 70 percent or greater chance of closing, whom I haven't called or emailed in the last week." Boom!

In all other cases, you seriously need to become a Close.io customer and see the immediate boost in sales success it will give your startup.

Why we developed sales software *for* sales people

Over 2 years ago, we started a "Sales As A Service" business called ElasticSales. The vision for Elastic was to build a massive sales infrastructure, and empower startups and companies around the world to tap into it in order to scale their sales effort.

Think Amazon AWS for Sales.

Our mission was simple: **Never again should a great company fail because of a lack of sales.**

We started hiring top sales talent, opening offices, and signing up clients within the first few weeks. It was clear that there was massive demand for this service out there. What wasn't clear was what kind of software we need to use to make this sales operation work smoothly.

We went out into the market to research the best available technologies and came back incredibly disappointed. Nothing out there was designed to actually help you sell more successfully.

All existing solutions seemed to be focused on the premise of turning sales professionals into manual "data-entry-monkeys". None of them showed any understanding whatsoever of what a sales person's needs are when it comes to their job and daily workflow.

After a lot of frustration, we decided to fix the problem instead of complaining about it and began developing our own internal sales application.

We lovingly called it our secret sales sauce ☺.

We knew nobody had ever been in a better position to develop next generation sales software since we had a few unfair competitive advantages:

- We had both salespeople and engineers on the founding team.
- We ran a sales outsourcing and consultancy firm for startups,

empowering us to test the software in all kinds of different use cases.

- We had a clear and distinct philosophy and vision for the product.

All that translated in a few simple principles when we started developing our software:

- It had to be simple to use.
- It had to minimize manual data entry as much as possible.
- It had to be focused on the #1 priority in sales: good communication.

We wanted to build software that sales people would actually love. We wanted to build something WE WOULD LOVE.

It took nearly 1.5 years of constant development and iteration with our internal development and sales team to realize that early vision and create something truly special.

During that time, our sales people generated millions of dollars in sales for hundreds of venture-backed Silicon Valley startups by using our secret sales sauce: Close.io.

We knew we had a huge winner when we suddenly started to get more and more demand from other people who wanted to use our internal "secret-sauce-sales-software".

At first, we resisted (after all, there is a reason we called it our secret sauce) but eventually we realized it was the right thing to do in order to remain true to our core mission: **Never again should a great company fail because of a lack of sales.**

So we did it. In January 2013, we finally released Close.io to the world. And the response from the market has been incredible:

71

"Close.io is awesome! Moving over from Salesforce is mind-blowing. I just wanted to see something and found it immediately. Funny how that's an advantage. Keep it up!"—Joseph Walla, Founder & CEO, HelloFax

"The straightforward email and calling integration in Close.io helped us solve many of our workflow issues and increased our outreach by over 30%. This has caused us to achieve huge growth in revenues while doing less work!"—Nick Persico, Director of Sales Operations, Krossover

"Close.io radically increased the number of calls and emails to our leads by logging everything automatically so the reps can focus on talking not logging." —Jeff Zwelling, Co-Founder, Convertro & Co-Founder, EchoSign

Not too shabby, right?

But how exactly does that affect you?

Experience the Close.io magic yourself by trying a free, 14-day trial!

GET THE BONUS MATERIALS!

You've reached the end of the book, but I still have more for you:

- A simple checklist to always deliver winning product demos
- Free access to my 1-hour Product Demo Online Crash Course recording
- An exclusive recording between Hiten Shah, Kissmetrics, Crazy Egg and Quicksprout Co-Founder, and me on product demos

Claim all your free bonus materials here:
http://resources.close.io/productdemos

Want more startup sales advice?

Visit http://close.io/free-sales-course

Questions, comments? Just contact me at steli@close.io. I would love to hear from you!